Mary Magdalene's Easter Story

Mary Magdalene visits the empty tomb
John 20:10–18 for children

Written by Sara Hartman • Illustrated by Ed Koehler

CONCORDIA PUBLISHING HOUSE • SAINT LOUIS

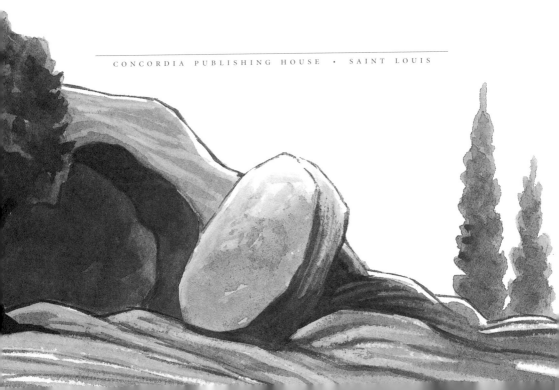

With eyes filled with tears,
And footsteps so slow,
Mary of Magdalene
Knew where she must go.

The Friday before
At the foot of His cross,
Mary saw Jesus die.
Now she felt a great loss.

As she walked toward the place
Where His body now lay,
Mary remembered how Jesus
Had freed her one day

From demons that bothered her
Year after year.
As she thought of His kindness,
She smiled through her tears.

She had traveled with Jesus,
His disciples and others.
Jesus treated them all
As sisters and brothers.

She remembered how Jesus
Had preached about love,
How He'd healed the sick,
Explained heaven above.

"But now it's all over,"
Mary thought with a sigh.
"Oh, why did He leave us?
Oh, why did He die?"

Mary stopped walking.
She had come to the cave
Where Jesus was sealed
In a cold, stony grave.

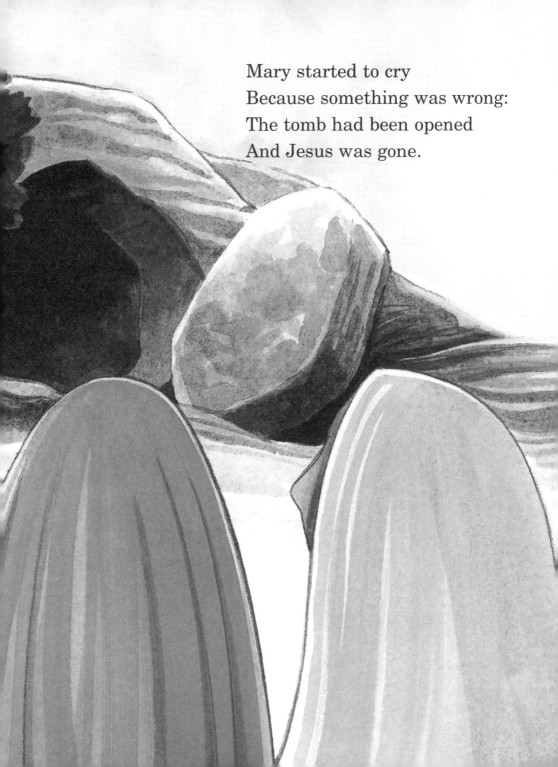

Mary started to cry
Because something was wrong:
The tomb had been opened
And Jesus was gone.

Two angels inside
Asked, "Why do you weep?"
And a man near Mary
Asked, "Whom do you seek?"

"I look for my Lord,"
She said in despair.
"His body's been taken.
Perhaps you know where?"

The man answered, "Mary."
When she heard His voice,
She looked up to see Jesus.
How her heart did rejoice!

"Teacher!" cried Mary,
"Is it really You?"
Jesus answered her gently,
"There is more I must do.

"I must go to My Father,
Who is your Father too.
Go tell My disciples
What you've seen here is true."

She obeyed right away
And ran to the place
Where the disciples had gathered.
Mary told of God's grace:

"God is great! He is mighty!
He fulfills all our needs!
Jesus lives! He is risen—
He is risen, indeed!"

Dear Parents,

Amid the turmoil and confusion of Jesus' last week on earth, Mary Magdalene stayed near Him. She traveled with Jesus and His disciples on the journey to Jerusalem and was in the crowd on Palm Sunday. She was likely present at Jesus' trial and torture and certainly was in the crowd at His crucifixion (John 19:25). Mary Magdalene did what she could to care for Jesus in His, life (Luke 8:2–3), and she continued in her devoted care after His death—"on the first day of the week, . . . Mary Magdalene went to the tomb" (John 20:1) to observe the Jewish tradition and anoint His body with spices.

In Mary Magdalene, we have a picture of Jesus' work in our lives. He had cast demons (Mark 16:9) from her, providing her with His forgiveness and healing. Mary's response was a life of devotion to her Savior. She followed, listened, learned, and served in His name. And when she learned about His victory over death and resurrection from the grave, she ran to spread the news.

This Easter, tell your child about Mary Magdalene. Talk about ways you can follow her example of faith and witness. And rejoice that He is risen!

The Editor